Germany
the people

Kathryn Lane

A Bobbie Kalman Book

The Lands, Peoples, and Cultures Series

Crabtree Publishing Company

www.crabtreebooks.com

The Lands, Peoples, and Cultures Series

Created by Bobbie Kalman

Coordinating editor
Ellen Rodger

Project editor
Lisa Gurusinghe

Production coordinator
Rosie Gowsell

Project development, photo research, and design
First Folio Resource Group, Inc.
 Erinn Banting
 Pauline Beggs
 Tom Dart
 Bruce Krever
 Debbie Smith

Editing
Jessica Rudolph

Separations and film
Embassy Graphics

Printer
Worzalla Publishing Company

Consultants
Sandra Schier, The Goethe Institute; Sonja Schlegel,
Consulate General of Germany

Photographs
Archiv/Photo Researchers: p. 10 (left); Archive
Photos: p. 8, p. 9 (top), p. 11; Corbis/AFP: p. 13;
Corbis/James L. Amos: p. 20 (top); Corbis/Bettmann:
p. 7 (both), p. 12 (both), p. 26 (bottom); Corbis/Ric
Ergenbright: p. 28 (top); Corbis/Owen Franken: title
page; Corbis/Marc Garanger: p. 30 (bottom); Corbis/
Dave G. Houser: p. 23 (bottom); Corbis/Bob Krist:
cover, p. 15 (bottom), p. 23 (top); Corbis/Becky
Luigart-Stayner: p. 22 (right); Corbis/Jim McDonald:
p. 20 (bottom); Corbis/Steve Raymer: p. 28 (bottom);
Corbis/Paul A. Souders: p. 4 (bottom); Corbis/Adam
Wolfitt: p. 22 (left), p. 29 (left); Corbis/Jenny
Woodcock; Reflections Photo Library: p. 30 (top);
Corbis/Michael S. Yamashita: p. 24 (bottom), p. 25;
Reinhard Feisel: p. 21 (bottom); Giraudon/Art
Resource: p. 6 (right); Beryl Goldberg: p. 4 (top), p. 14
(both), p. 17 (top), p. 27 (both), p. 31; Tom & Michelle
Grimm/International Stock: p. 19 (bottom); The
Hulton-Getty Picture Library/Archive Photos: p. 9
(bottom); Jan Lukas/Photo Researchers: p. 10 (right);
David Peevers: p. 3, p. 5 (all), p. 6 (left), p. 15 (top),
p. 16 (both), p. 17 (bottom), p. 18 (both), p. 19 (top),
p. 21 (top), p. 24 (top), p. 29 (right); Ulrike Welsch/
Photo Researchers: p. 26 (top)

Illustrations
Dianne Eastman: icon
David Wysotski, Allure Illustrations: back cover

Cover: Two friends chat before a parade in Munich,
in Southen Germany.

Title page: A group of children sit together on a bus
during a field trip in Dresden, a city in eastern
Germany.

Icon: A half-timbered house, which is built by filling
a wooden frame with white plaster, appears at the
head of each section.

Back cover: The *Heidschnucken*, a type of sheep found
in parts of northern Germany, has long, straggly
wool and curled horns.

Note: When using foreign terms, the author has
followed the German style of capitalizing all nouns,
regardless of where they appear in a sentence.

Published by
Crabtree Publishing Company

PMB 16A,	612 Welland Avenue	73 Lime Walk
350 Fifth Avenue	St. Catharines	Headington
Suite 3308	Ontario, Canada	Oxford OX3 7AD
New York, NY	L2M 5V6	United Kingdom
10118		

LC

Cataloging-in-Publication Data
Lane, Kathryn, 1969–
   Germany : The people / Kathryn Lane.
   p. cm. -- (The lands, peoples, and cultures series)
   Includes index.
   ISBN 0-7787-9373-7 (RLB) -- ISBN 0-7787-9741-4 (pbk.)
   1. Germany--Social life and customs--Juvenile literature. 2.
Minorities--Germany--Juvenile literature. 3. Germany--History--
Juvenile literature. [1. Germany--Social life and customs. 2.
Germany--History.] I. Title. II. Series.
DD61 .L322 2001
943--dc21
                          00-069352
                          LC

Contents

A ride through Germany

Imagine bicycling down a busy street in a large German city. People hurry past, carrying briefcases and talking on cell phones. Tall, modern buildings tower above. You ride out of town, past neat suburbs and massive factories, past fields and farms, until you reach a small village. Here, things move at a slower pace. Regulars sit in the local **pub**, and people tend their gardens. Many of the houses are hundreds of years old. You stop to watch traditional dancers practicing for the harvest festival. As a treat, you buy yourself a slice of apple strudel, a delicious, flaky pastry, to give you energy for the ride back to the city.

(right) A woman chats with her friend while pushing a baby carriage on a busy street in Frankfurt am Main, a city in the west.

(below) A family enjoys a picnic in Bavaria, a region in the south of Germany.

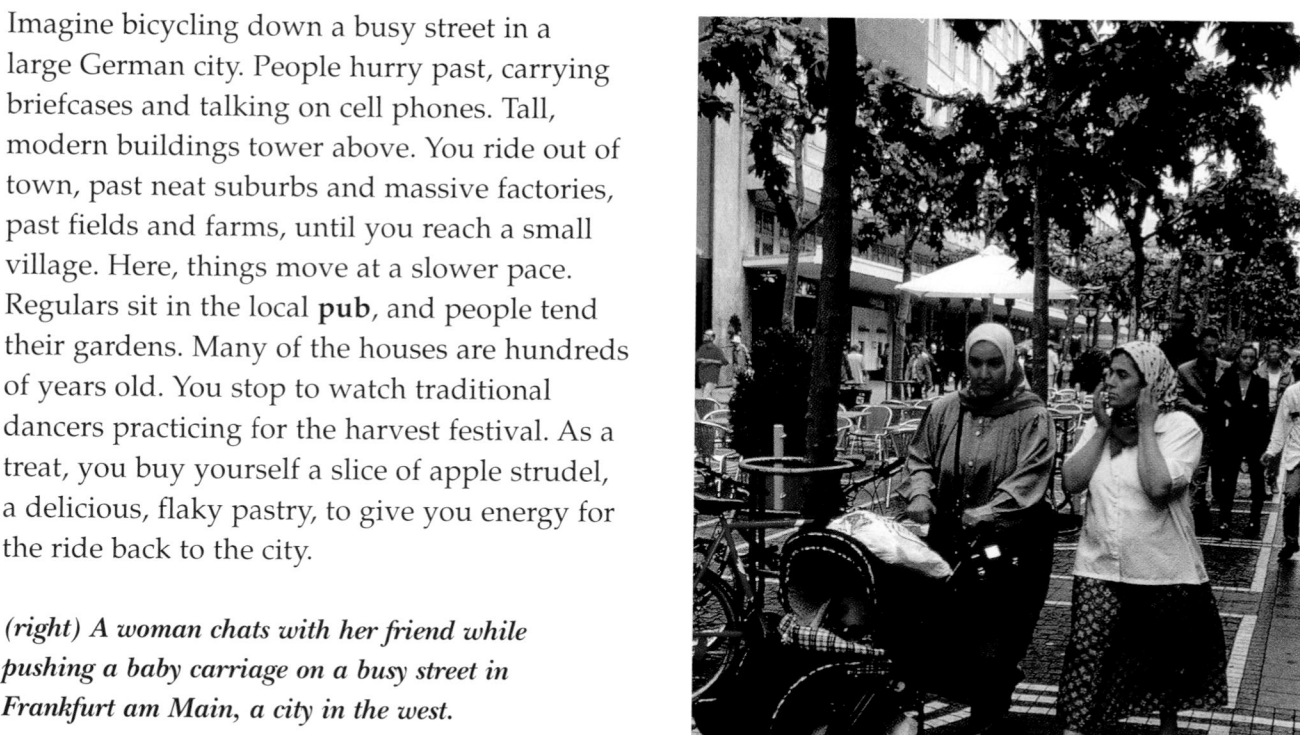

A time of change

Germany is a land with many regions. Each region has its own traditions, which have been passed down for generations. During the past hundred years, Germany has experienced enormous changes. Much of the 1900s were marred by war and hardship. From 1945 to 1989, the country was split in two. Today, Germany is a **unified** country again. Its people are working together to make sure that it is a place of opportunity for everyone.

A farmer on the island of Rügen, off the northern coast of Germany, takes his horses to the blacksmith to get new horseshoes.

Friends take a break from their soccer game in Wismar, a city in the north.

A market in Berlin sells bananas, tangerines, strawberries, and other tasty fruit.

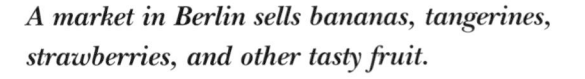

Around 1200 B.C., a group of people called the Celts lived in the southern part of the land that became Germany. They developed the use of iron to make tools and weapons.

Around 300 B.C., different Germanic peoples, such as the Vandals, Franks, Goths, Saxons, and Cherusci, started moving into the lands that are now Germany. They came from the areas north of present day Sweden and Denmark. After battles and wars with the Germanic peoples, the Celts were forced to move. The Germanic peoples settled on their land, farming and raising cattle.

(above) Two Roman warriors battle in this mosaic from an ancient Roman villa, in what is now Germany.

(right) Charlemagne (742–814) was a daring warrior and a strong leader of the Frankish Empire.

The Romans

By 9 A.D., Roman armies had conquered much of Europe, the Middle East, and the north coast of Africa. They had already reached the Rhine River, in what is now western Germany. When the Romans tried to cross the Rhine, they met with opposition from the Germanic peoples, led by a prince named Arminius. The huge Roman armies were defeated at the Battle of Teutoburg. After this defeat, the Romans stayed in the areas they already **occupied** around the Rhine and Danube Rivers. They did not try to spread further into Germanic lands. They built the first vineyards along the Rhine and started many German towns that still exist today, including Cologne and Regensburg.

Charlemagne

The Franks became the most powerful of the Germanic peoples. Their king, Charlemagne, ruled the Frankish Empire, which covered most of Western Europe. He encouraged learning and spread his religion, **Christianity**, throughout the empire. Charlemagne developed a strong relationship with Pope Leo III, the head of the **Roman Catholic Church**. Together, they worked to keep peace in the Frankish Empire.

Dividing the empire

The Frankish Empire was later divided into western and eastern parts. The western part was made up mostly of French-speaking people. It covered about the same area as modern day France. The eastern part was made up mostly of German-speaking people. It included today's Germany, Austria, and Switzerland, and parts of Italy, France, Belgium, and the Netherlands.

The Empire's many names

The eastern part of the early Frankish Empire had many names. So did its rulers. Conrad I, crowned in 911, is considered the first German king. His rule marks the time when the area became known as the German *Reich*, which means kingdom or realm. Beginning in 962 the kings became known as emperors. The title of emperor was given by the pope. By the 1000s, the area was known as the Roman Empire. In the 1200s, it was called the Holy Roman Empire and by the 1400s, the full name was the Holy Roman Empire of the German Nation.

Louis and Charles, the grandsons of Charlemagne, ruled two separate parts of the divided Frankish Empire. In 842, they united their kingdoms to protect their lands from invasion.

Time of the knights

Shortly before 1100 A.D., armies of Christians headed east to fight crusades, which were wars against people with different religious beliefs. In 1190, a group of German crusaders started the Order of Teutonic Knights. Knights were skilled warriors who had been specially trained in fighting and horseback riding.

After the crusades, the Order of Teutonic Knights concentrated on **converting** the people of Eastern Europe to Roman Catholicism and gaining territory for the Church and themselves. The Teutonic Knights became powerful. They ruled over a great area of land until their defeat in the early 1400s. Today, the Teutonic Order is mainly a religious order. Its headquarter is in Vienna, Austria. It has set up many hospitals and centers for the homeless in Eastern Europe.

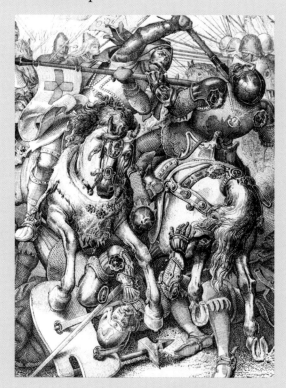

Knights took a vow of chivalry. They swore that they would protect women, fight for the weak, and spread the Roman Catholic religion.

The Holy Roman Empire of the German Nation was made up of many regions. The regions were ruled by dukes and princes. The emperors felt that the dukes and princes threatened their own power and the unity of the empire. They tried to lessen the influence of the regional rulers. In spite of their efforts, many of the regions grew rich and powerful.

Martin Luther

Martin Luther (1483–1546) was a monk, a religious man who dedicated his life to **worship** and study. He used simple and clear language to teach Christians what they should believe and how they should live their lives. He also translated the Bible from the ancient Latin language into German so that everyone could understand it.

Luther spoke out against what he saw as the power and dishonesty of the Roman Catholic Church, especially the selling of "indulgences." People bought indulgences to have their sins, or misdeeds, forgiven. They received a piece of paper, or receipt, that said they had confessed their sins, they were sorry, and they had been forgiven. The practice of selling indulgences went against Luther's belief that people's actions were not what made them good in the eyes of God; goodness was God's blessing. Luther was also angry that the Church used the money it made from indulgences to pay for the luxurious lifestyles of the Church leaders, while most common people lived in poverty. Luther and his followers became known as Protestants, which means "those who protest."

The Thirty Years' War

Some of the dukes and princes who ruled the regions in the Holy Roman Empire of the German Nation supported the Protestants. Other regional rulers supported the Roman Catholic Church and the emperor. The Catholics and Protestants struggled for power over many decades. From 1618 to 1648, the confusion led to a terrible war that lasted thirty years. By the end of the Thirty Years' War, the emperor held very little power and the empire was divided into more than 300 tiny states.

Two Catholic officials are thrown from a palace window by Protestant rebels. This incident began the Thirty Years' War.

After 1871, Bismarck's goal was to keep peace in the newly united German Empire.

Germany united

During the 1700s and 1800s, the northeastern state of Prussia and its capital, Berlin, grew in power. The *Kaiser*, or king, of Prussia, Wilhelm I, made Otto von Bismarck the chancellor of Prussia in 1862. The job of chancellor was similar to that of a president or prime minister.

Bismarck was determined to bring all German peoples under the power of Prussia. He involved his state in many short wars. With each war, he managed to gain territory or convince other states to join Prussia. By 1871, he had succeeded in uniting many states, and the country became known as the German Empire.

The Great War

In June 1914, the Crown Prince of Austria was assassinated, or murdered for political reasons. When the Austro-Hungarian Empire, of which Austria was part, declared war on the countries it held responsible for the assassination, Germany supported its neighbor and entered World War I. Germany fought against the Allied Forces, also called the Allies. The Allies included soldiers from many countries, such as France, Britain, Russia, Canada, and the United States. In 1918, World War I ended. It became known as the Great War because people from so many countries were involved. Sixty-five million people fought in the war. Ten million, including over a million **civilians**, died.

The Treaty of Versailles

Germany was forced to sign the Treaty of Versailles. Under this agreement, Germany lost large areas of land and was not allowed to rebuild its military. The treaty said that Germany was to blame for the war and was responsible for all the damage that the war had caused. Germany had to make huge payments to the Allies. These payments left Germany's **economy** in ruins.

After World War I, inflation made prices in Germany rise. The German currency, the **deutschmark,** *became so worthless that children used it to make kites.*

Germans salute Adolf Hitler, who was elected chancellor in 1933.

In the 1930s, the Great Depression, a worldwide economic crisis, hit Germany. The German government seemed unable to help its people during these difficult times.

The rise of Hitler

Adolf Hitler, the leader of a small political party called the National Socialist or Nazi party, claimed he could solve Germany's problems. In his passionate speeches, he insisted that Germany should not make payments to the Allies. He also said that the land lost with the signing of the Treaty of Versailles should be taken back, and that all German-speaking people, including those living in other countries, should be united.

The "master race"

One of Hitler's main beliefs was that ethnic Germans, the **descendants** of the Germanic peoples who began living on the land around 300 B.C., belonged to a "master race." Hitler believed that ethnic Germans were better than all other human beings. He blamed many of Germany's problems on the Jews and spread hatred against them throughout the country. Jews lost their rights. They were not allowed to vote, inherit land, or travel freely. Jews suffered terrible attacks of organized violence. They were assaulted in the streets and their houses of worship, called synagogues, were burned to the ground.

Under the Nazis

Once in power, the Nazis moved quickly to make Germany a **dictatorship**. They banned all other political parties. Violence was used against people who publicly disagreed with the Nazis. Hitler made himself the all-powerful *Führer*, or leader. Hitler's Nazi ideas were taught in schools and at meetings of youth groups that all Christian Germans between the ages of ten and eighteen had to join.

Preparing for war

While Hitler was in power, the economy grew stronger. Many people found jobs building the *Autobahn*, a huge network of highways. They also went to work making weapons of war. According to the Treaty of Versailles, Germany was not allowed to build up their weapon supply. Hitler was preparing for war, something the Treaty was supposed to prevent.

Under Hitler's rule, Jews were forced to wear yellow stars on their clothing so people could identify them.

World War II begins

Hitler began to put into practice his dream of uniting all Germans and acquiring more land for Germany. During 1938 and 1939, he invaded Austria and then Czechoslovakia. When he invaded Poland in 1939, France and Britain declared war to try to stop Germany from taking over other countries. Germany was well prepared for war. It defeated Poland and then took over Belgium, the Netherlands, Denmark, Norway, and France by the summer of 1940. By 1942, World War II had spread throughout much of the world.

The Holocaust

During World War II, the Nazis murdered six million Jews, one third of all Jews in the world. This well-planned mass murder is known as the Holocaust. Jews in every country occupied by the Nazis were rounded up and sent to concentration camps. In these camps, healthy adults were used for slave labor and were often worked to death. Children, the sick, and the elderly, who were not suitable for labor, were murdered soon after their arrival. They were locked in large rooms, called gas chambers, and killed by poisonous cyanide gas. In the gas chambers, up to one thousand people could be murdered at once. Most of Europe's Romany peoples and many homosexuals, political opponents, and mentally and physically disabled people were also murdered during the Holocaust.

The end of the war

In 1943, Germany tried to invade the Soviet Union. The enormous size of the Soviet Union, the brutal winter, and Soviet people's determination to fight, were too much for the German soldiers. Germany suffered one of its worst military defeats. From then on, German forces were slowly pushed out of the countries they had invaded. By 1945, Germany itself was occupied by the Allies. Many of its towns and cities had been heavily bombed and much of the country lay in rubble. While the country was being overrun by enemy troops, Hitler killed himself in an underground bomb shelter.

Anti-Semitism and nationalism

Hitler did not invent the hatred of Jews, known as anti-Semitism. Anti-Semitism has a long history in Europe. It is based on lies that have been passed down for centuries. Jews were thrown out of many European countries between 1300 and 1500. From the 1700s to the early 1900s, many Jews were killed in Eastern Europe during organized **massacres** called pogroms. Until the mid-1900s, Eastern European Jews were forced to live in ghettos, separate cramped and dirty areas of cities that were sometimes surrounded by a wall.

The idea of nationalism, or loyalty to a person's country, became popular in the 1800s. Nationalists in any country feel connected to one another by their common ancestors, language, and culture. Fellow citizens who do not share the nationalists' culture or ethnic background are treated as outsiders. The Nazis used the anti-Semitism and nationalism that already existed in Germany to gain support for their policies.

Cologne's cathedral and most of the surrounding buildings lay in ruins after the heavy bombing during World War II.

Division and reunification

After the war, control of Germany was divided among four of the Allied Forces — Britain, France, the Soviet Union, and the United States. The Federal Republic of Germany, or West Germany, was created when Britain, France, and the United States joined their sections. The Soviet section became the German Democratic Republic, or East Germany. The border between East and West Germany was well guarded and marked by a fence. East and West Germans had to show passports any time they wanted to cross into the other country.

The former capital, Berlin, was also divided between East and West Germany. East Berlin became the capital of East Germany, and Bonn became the capital of West Germany.

The Marshall Plan

Between 1948 and 1952, western Germany received over $1.4 billion in aid from the United States. This program of financial assistance, called the Marshall Plan, was meant to help the economy after the war. It succeeded. During the 1950s, West Germany's economy boomed. East Germany's economy grew more slowly. The country's Soviet government was involved in what was called the Cold War. It had broken almost all contact with the western world and refused the money the U.S. offered.

East and West

Many East Germans began to move to West Germany, looking for better jobs and more money. They were also trying to escape their government's strict control and find more freedom than they had in their own country. By the 1960s, 20,000 East Germans were moving to West Germany each month, usually by crossing from East Berlin into West Berlin. The East German government considered all these people leaving to be a threat to the country's existence. In the middle of the night, on August 13, 1961, 40,000 men closed streets and sealed the border between the east and west parts of Berlin. Within days, a 103-mile (165-kilometer) wall surrounded West Berlin.

(above) Konrad Adenauer was the first chancellor of West Germany and one of the politicians to sign The Basic Law in 1949. This law included many terms designed to protect West Germany's democracy.

(left) People gather at a ceremony in western Germany to celebrate the purchase of 75 new freight cars with money from The Marshall Plan.

The great divide

The East German authorities made sure that the border was completely sealed. Barbed-wire fences were set up in the water where the border ran across rivers. Where the border ran through the middle of buildings, they were boarded up, forcing families out of their homes. At first, there was no communication between people on either side of the Wall. Even letters could not be mailed to the other side. By 1963, West Berliners were allowed to cross at one of two checkpoints for brief visits with relatives in the East. Most East Germans, on the other hand, could not leave their country.

Escaping to the West

Many East Germans tried to escape to West Berlin. Some succeeded, but 80 people were killed by East Berlin border guards, and many others were sent to prison.

Those who escaped usually went through tunnels that started in people's basements and snaked under the Berlin Wall to West Berlin. One East German family was especially resourceful. Over several months, family members bought many small pieces of nylon material. They painstakingly sewed the pieces together, creating a hot air balloon. They had just enough fuel to get into the air, and then simply glided into West Berlin. Luckily, the wind was blowing in the right direction.

Tearing down the wall

In the late 1980s, East Germans began to demand more freedom. In October 1989, they held huge protests against their government. Finally, on November 9, 1989, the East German government lifted the border restrictions they had imposed 28 years before. East Berliners poured across the opened checkpoints. A huge party broke out in the streets. With the help of East German border guards, many Berliners started breaking down the Wall with pickaxes and chisels.

Reunification

By October 3, 1990, the official date of reunification, the West German government had become the government of a reunited Germany. Despite everyone's initial optimism, reunification has been difficult. Many East Germans lost their jobs when the outdated factories where they worked were forced to close. They also lost many of their social programs, including free childcare. Living costs, such as rent, have become much higher. West Germans' taxes were raised to help pay for the cost of modernizing the former East Germany's industries, transportation routes, and telephone lines. Although times are difficult, Germans are working together to rebuild their country.

East German border guards stand behind a section of the Berlin Wall that is being removed by West German soldiers in 1989.

 # The people

Most of the 82 million people living in Germany are ethnic Germans. They can trace their roots back to the people who settled in the area around 300 B.C. A small group of people called the Sorbs have also lived in Germany for centuries. They settled on the eastern border in the 500s and speak a language called Sorbian.

Other people have come to Germany more recently. People from countries such as Turkey, India, and Yugoslavia moved to Germany in the 1960s to look for work. More Yugoslavians came in the 1990s, escaping war in their homeland. Still more people came to West Germany in the 1980s from Eastern European countries, such as Russia, Czechoslovakia, Poland, and Romania, when these countries opened their borders and people were able to travel to the west.

A grocer reads a newspaper outside his store while waiting for customers.

Belonging to a region

Throughout their history, ethnic Germans thought of themselves as belonging to a region, such as Bavaria or Prussia, rather than to a country as a whole. Even today, Germans are more likely to identify with the region in which they live.

Each region has its own traditions, type of clothing, typical foods, and local dialect, or version, of the German language. Not only are words pronounced differently in different parts of the country, but there are often different words for the same thing. For example, bread rolls, a common food all over the country, are called *Semmeln* in the south and *Brötchen* in the north.

Three friends in Lubeck, a city in northern Germany, chat after school.

Friends and family take a break after a long walk in Berlin.

A man wears a traditional hat, decorated with a huge feather and a bunch of flowers, at a festival in Bavaria.

Gastarbeiter

Many people who moved to Germany in the 1960s from countries such as Turkey, Greece, Yugoslavia, and Italy came to fill low-paying jobs that West Germans were not interested in taking. They were known as "guest workers," or *Gastarbeiter*. They were expected to move back to their countries after a few years. Instead, many stayed and had children. After the economy worsened during the 1970s and unemployment rose, some Germans thought the foreign workers were taking jobs away from the citizens of the country. Some of these workers suffered violence and **discrimination**. Such violence against immigrants still breaks out from time to time, particularly in the former East Germany, where poverty and unemployment are higher than in the western part of the country.

Turks

More than two million immigrants and their descendants from Turkey, live in Germany. They are the largest non-German community in the country. Many came to Germany seeking work in the 1960s and 1970s and had children there. The younger people of the Turkish community think of Germany as their home. They often speak German instead of Turkish, which their parents speak. Many of Germany's large cities have a Turkish neighborhood with Turkish restaurants, signs, and shops. In fact, the Turkish meat sandwich, *Döner Kebab*, has become the most popular fast food in the country.

 # Living in the cities

Germany's cities are fast-paced and exciting. Shoppers crowd into outdoor markets and traffic jams the streets. Café patios are packed with people watching the action around them. Most Germans live in cities or in the **suburbs**. They like to live near their work and enjoy the many conveniences and events, such as plays and art shows, that take place close by.

Nearly every city in Germany has its own fairs or festivals, with merry-go-rounds, fast-food booths, and craft exhibits. Some festivals have been celebrated for hundreds of years, while others started more recently.

Rebuilding the cities

During World War II, bombs destroyed many of Germany's cities. Some had to be completely rebuilt. These cities are modern looking, with tall skyscrapers, apartment buildings, and wide roads. Other cities carefully rebuilt their bombed buildings so that they look the same as they did long ago. Still other cities were lucky enough to have the *Altstadt*, the old city, escape the bombs. These neighborhoods have narrow, cobbled streets that twist between buildings that are hundreds of years old.

(left) People gather for a festival in the Town Hall Square in Kiel, a city in northern Germany.

(below) Modern apartment buildings and businesses crowd the downtown streets of Hamburg.

Three friends ride their bikes along the Saar River in Saarbrücken, in the east.

People stroll through a **Fussgänger Zone,** *or pedestrian area, in the center of Bacharach, in the west.*

Apartment living

In German cities houses tend to be very expensive, so most people rent apartments instead. Some neighborhoods, are made up almost entirely of apartment buildings. Sometimes people own a small plot of land near their apartment, where they grow fruit and vegetables. They may even build a small hut on it and use it as a cottage in the summer.

Getting around

Germans who live in cities are encouraged to leave their cars at home and ride public transportation or a bicycle instead. Some cities have a program called "park and ride." It allows people who live in nearby towns or in the suburbs to park their cars outside the city, and take a bus around town for free. These buses usually run every hour, so people can use the "park and ride" to get in or out of the city whenever they want. People who try to drive in the city quickly discover that it can be very difficult to find a place to park. Even if there is a place to park, it is usually very expensive to park for the day.

In some downtown sections, there is a pedestrian area called a *Fussgänger Zone*. No cars, buses, or taxis are permitted in this area. Trucks are only allowed on the street to deliver to neighborhood shops during certain times, such as early in the morning. Germany's "no car" policies relieve traffic delays and help the environment by cutting down on pollution.

 # Village life

Villages dot the countryside throughout Germany. Many have beautiful old houses and winding streets. Some are still surrounded by the walls that protected the villagers from enemy attacks hundreds of years ago. Life in a village is more social so the pace seems slower. People chat in the town square where farmers from the area sell their produce at market stalls.

Working

Some people who live in villages commute to work in the factories and offices of nearby cities. Others work on farms. Some do both, waking up early to do farm chores before going to work in the city, then returning home to do chores in the evening. Many villagers also create traditional crafts. For example, in the Black Forest in the southwest, craftspeople are famous for building cuckoo clocks. In Erzebirge, in the east, they build brightly painted wooden toys.

Local festivals

Some villages hold festivals based on local historical events or special times of the year such as the grape harvest. Almost everyone participates in them. Villagers dress in local costumes, musicians play traditional instruments, and dance troupes perform regional dances. Tourists and people from the area gather in the village to enjoy the festivities.

(left) People stroll through the narrow streets of Rothenburg, a medieval village in southern Germany.

(top) A village sits on the shores of Lake Fulda, in the north.

Richtfest

Traditions tend to be maintained longer in villages than in big cities. One tradition involves a party called a *Richtfest*. A *Richtfest* is held when a house is half built, with the wooden frame standing without brick and plaster on the walls. This party celebrates the end of the first major step of making a house. All those involved in the construction are invited. Guests bring gifts of bread and salt, and a small evergreen wreath is set on the roof for good luck. For the carpenters who made the wooden frame, the *Richtfest* is a kind of farewell party. Their part of the work is now done.

Half-timbered houses

Half-timbered houses are common in Germany. Builders construct a wooden frame and then fill in the spaces between the pieces of wood with white plaster. The frame, which is still visible on the outside of the house, is then painted black so it stands out against the white plaster. Originally, the plaster was meant to be temporary. Once the house owner had saved enough money, he or she would replace the plaster with stones. Such a person was said to be *steinreich*, or "stone rich."

Years ago, half-timbered houses had roofs made of grasses woven together tightly. These roofs wore out quickly and caught fire easily. Today, half-timbered houses have shingled roofs.

Farmhouses

In the **foothills** of the southwest, large wooden farmhouses dot the countryside. These houses have wide, gradually sloping roofs that almost reach the ground. Carefully carved balconies, often decorated with flowers, stretch across the second floor. These houses are sturdy and warm. They only have a few small windows because larger windows allow drafts from winter winds to blow inside.

Many Black Forest homes have sloped roofs to allow snow to slide off in the winter.

 # Celebration time!

In Germany, as in other countries, there are special festivities to mark a new stage in a person's life. Birthday parties, wedding receptions, and other celebrations give friends and relatives a chance to congratulate one another and to see each other at joyous times.

Happy birthday!

Much like children in North America, German children look forward to their birthday for weeks before it arrives. On their special day, they invite friends to their house for a party with snacks and games. When the guests arrive, they place their gifts in a pile on the birthday table. A candleholder with a candle for each year of the child's life sits on the birthday table as well. As the guests sing *"Zum Geburtstag viel Glück"* or "good luck for your birthday", or sometimes "Happy Birthday" in English, the birthday girl or boy makes a wish and blows out the candles.

Party games

In one favorite birthday party game, a large piece of chocolate, a silly hat, a pair of gloves, a knife, and a fork are placed in the middle of a table. Players sit around the table and take turns rolling a die. Whoever rolls a six puts on the hat and gloves quickly and begins to eat the chocolate using the knife and fork. The other players continue to roll the die. If someone else rolls a six, that person puts on the hat and gloves and begins eating the chocolate, sometimes before the last person even has a chance to start!

(right) A boy blows up a balloon at a birthday party.

(top) A Roman Catholic priest baptizes a girl in Frankfurt am Main. A baptism is a ceremony that welcomes a person into the Roman Catholic Church.

20

A couple heads to their wedding reception while a band plays music behind them.

Getting married

All couples get married at city hall, though some choose to have a religious ceremony afterwards in a church or other house of worship. The couple exchanges rings, but they wear the rings on their right hands, not on their left as North Americans do. After the wedding, there is often a huge party for friends and family.

To work!

Deciding to get married in Germany means a lot of hard work for the future bride and groom. Friends and relatives present the couple with all sorts of tasks to prove that they can work together. Before the wedding, guests come to a party called a *Polterabend* with old dishes and flowerpots. Throughout the evening, the guests smash the dishes on the floor. The noise is said to scare away evil spirits. People also believe that the smaller the broken pieces, the more luck the couple will have. If the couple manages to clean up the mess, it is hoped that they will be able to deal with any difficult situations that occur when they are married.

Sawing a log

The bride and groom's work continues after the wedding. At a traditional wedding in the south, the couple might come out of the church to find a sawhorse with a large log lying across it. The bride and groom each take one end of a long saw and together cut the log in half.

Returning home

In northern Germany, guests sometimes play a trick on the newlyweds. When the bride and groom return home from the church, they find all their doors are blocked. If they live in a house, all their furniture is on the roof! First, the couple has to find a way into their home. Then, they have to bring all the furniture back inside. A large crowd usually gathers on the street to watch the couple struggle, but nobody is allowed to lend a hand!

Sawing logs is a difficult, sweaty job— especially when the bride is wearing a long, flowing wedding gown and the groom is wearing a suit!

Hungry?

Traditional German food is rich and hearty. Meat and potatoes are typical of the German diet. Germans love food from other countries too, such as a Chinese stir-fry and Italian pizza.

Meals

In Germany, lunch is the main meal of the day. It is usually served hot and often includes vegetables, roast chicken or *Schnitzel*, which is a cutlet often made from pork and *Knödel*, chewy potato dumplings, or *Spätzle*, fat, thick noodles. Breakfast and dinner are generally lighter meals. They tend to include German bread, often made from a type of grain called rye, and different kinds of cheese. Cheese, fruit, and sausages or other cold meats are also part of these meals.

In Germany, all sorts of vegetables, from peppers to mushrooms, are pickled.

A couple eats lunch in the Viktualienmarkt, the main food market in Munich.

Pickling food

Before the invention of refrigerators, pickling, or soaking food in salt water or vinegar, was a popular way to preserve food. The food was sealed in a jar with brine or vinegar for anywhere from two weeks to several months.

During the 1700s, Frederick the Great of Prussia had a monopoly on salt which meant that all salt had to be bought from him. To make sure that the salt trade made a lot of money, everyone who lived in the capital, Berlin, had to buy large amounts of salt, even if they needed it. People started pickling everything they could think of just to use the extra salt. These cooks invented many dishes that are still favorites in Germany. *Sauerkraut*, which is pickled shredded cabbage, is a tart side dish that goes well with meat. *Rollmops*, pickled fish wrapped around pickled cucumbers, or dill pickles, is a popular snack in the north, where seafood is often eaten. *Sauerbraten*, or **braised** pickled beef, is another favorite dish.

Sausages

Germany is well known for its sausages. There are over 300 kinds! Many regions and cities have their own specialties. Although most sausages are made from pork, each type tastes different. *Bratwurst*, which are grilled pork sausages, are the most common sausages in Germany. *Weisswurst*, or white sausages, come from the south and are made of veal. *Knackwurst* are plump sausages that get their name from the cracking sound their splitting skins make when they are heated. In Berlin and in the Ruhr region, *Currywurst* are a favorite. These pork sausages are served drenched in a spicy ketchup-and-curry sauce.

In southern Germany, *Wurstküchen* are restaurants that serve nothing but sausages. At a street food stall called an *Imbiss*, there are a number of different sausages to choose from. Cooked on an open grill and served in a long bun, sausages taste best when smothered in another German specialty — mustard!

A chef takes a break after putting out a variety of bread, meat, and cheese for lunch at his restaurant in Berlin.

*A vendor cooks sausages at an **Imbiss** in Nuremburg, in southern Germany.*

Döner Kebabs

During the 1970s, Turkish immigrants opened up stalls selling *Döner Kebabs*. Over the years, these sandwiches have grown in popularity. Thin pieces of meat are sliced from a larger piece of meat cooked on a rotating skewer. They are then stuffed into a flatbread pocket. Raw vegetables are added to the sandwich, with a generous squirt of yogurt sauce and a shake of extra hot spice to top it off. A *Döner Kebab* is delicious and very messy!

Pastries

Meeting friends at a *Konditorei*, or pastry shop, is a popular way to spend an afternoon. The *Konditorei* has many different treats, including rich cakes, handmade chocolates, and flaky pastries such as apple strudel. Bakers make their own creations, often using chocolate, whipped cream, sponge cake, and fruit preserves. A paste of ground almonds and sugar, called marzipan, and meringue, frothy baked egg whites sweetened with sugar are also used. *Schwarzwäelderkirschtorte*, or Black Forest cake, is popular throughout the country, with its delicious layers of chocolate sponge cake, cherry preserves, and whipped cream.

A bakery in Bacharach, in western Germany, sells pastries, cakes, cookies, and bread.

A confectioner, or person who makes candy, paints designs on marzipan.

Pfeffernuesse

A favorite snack in Germany is *Pfeffernuesse*, which means pepper nuts. With an adult's help, you can make these spicy cookies.

4 cups (1 L) all-purpose flour
1/2 cup (125 ml) white sugar
1 1/4 teaspoons (6 ml) baking soda
1/2 teaspoon (2 ml) nutmeg
1 1/2 teaspoons (7 ml) cinnamon
1/2 teaspoon (2 ml) cloves
black pepper
3/4 cup (180 ml) molasses
1/2 cup (125 ml) butter
2 eggs
icing sugar

1. Mix flour, sugar, baking soda, nutmeg, cinnamon, cloves, and black pepper in a large mixing bowl.

2. With the help of an adult, heat the molasses and butter in a pot.

3. Once the mixture melts, let it cool.

4. Add the eggs and the molasses mixture to the bowl. Mix well.

5. Cover the bowl and chill for several hours.

6. Make 1 inch (2.5 cm) balls with the mixture. Put them on a greased cookie sheet.

7. Bake at 350° F (180°C) for 12 to 14 minutes or until the cookies are golden brown.

8. Once the cookies are cool, cover with icing sugar.

Prost! Cheers!

Germany is famous for beer. There are over 1,000 breweries making hundreds of different kinds of beer, many of them particular to a region or city. These beers are made according to the *Reinheitsgebot*, Germany's purity law. This law, which dates back to 1516, is the oldest food law still in use. German beer contains no **preservatives** and is made from only water, **yeast**, and the grains barley and hops. The yeast causes the grain to **ferment**. Each beer gets its distinctive flavor from the method of brewing. In the city of Coburg, for example, brewers drop hot stones into fermenting beer. This causes the sugar in the grains to caramelize, or burn, changing the flavor.

Some cities, such as Munich, have massive beer gardens. Here, people eat sausages and roast chicken while sampling many types of beer. The beer is served in huge, heavy mugs with handles, called *Mass*.

Waitresses often carry up to four **Mass** *in each hand.*
Each **Mass** *contains two pints (one liter) of beer.*

A boy stands in front of the class during a spelling lesson.

Education has always been important in Germany. It was one of the first countries to have a nationwide school system, in which all children receive a quality education. From primary school right through to the end of university, school is free for all students.

A school day

Children begin school early in the morning, at 7:30 a.m. They spend the morning in classes, with one half-hour break, and are finished school by 1:00 p.m. Older students receive more homework than younger students. Once their homework is finished, many children spend the rest of the afternoon going to music classes, playing sports, or hanging around with their friends.

After *Grundschule*

From the age of six to ten, students attend primary school, called *Grundschule*. After *Grundschule*, they go to one of three schools. If they choose *Hauptschule*, they will finish when they are 15, then go on to vocational training. With vocational training, students spend part of their time at school and part-time at work training for a particular job. For example, they might learn about auto mechanics at a garage or about computers by working at a computer firm. Students usually work under the watchful eyes of a master of the trade or *Meister*.

Students who go to *Realschule* after *Grundschule* stay until they are 16. They must then take an exam to enter a college or they may choose vocational training instead.

Kindergarten

Friedrich Froebel (1782–1852) founded the first kindergarten in 1840. Kindergarten means "children's garden". Froebel thought that young children should be taught through play. He thought that it was important to keep them active and to make sure they were in a pleasant environment. He also suggested that teaching children ages three to six in such an informal way would help them better adjust to primary school. Froebel's ideas were completely new at the time. They became very popular, especially in North America.

Students look at a map during a field trip in Munich.

Gymnasium

The third type of school that children might go to after *Grundschule* is *Gymnasium*. *Gymnasium* lasts for at least nine years. After that time, the students must take a very difficult exam called an *Abitur*. All students who pass the *Abitur* can go to university, but some have to wait, since all available openings go to the best students.

Learning a language

Before reunification, all West German students learned English and French in addition to German, and all East German students studied Russian as a second language. Today, depending on the courses available at their school, German students can learn other languages as well.

During their early twenties, many young women go to another country for a year to work as an **au pair** or nanny. This gives them the opportunity to learn a new language or practice a language they learned at school.

National Service

All men are required to serve in the armed forces for ten months before they turn 25. They either go the *Bundeswehr*, or army, the *Bundesmarine*, or navy, the *Bundesluftwaffe*, or airforce. For the first three months, soldiers spend Monday to Friday at the army base. After three months, they can go home at night if they prefer. If people do not want to serve in the army, they can do thirteen months of community service instead. They might work in places such as hospitals or in homes for people with disabilities.

Learning a trade

Apprenticing, or learning a career from a professional, was a major part of education hundreds of years ago. To make sure that **artisans** were well trained, young people spent years working with a highly skilled person, called a *Meister*. The *Meister* passed on his skills to the apprentice.

After three years of learning with the *Meister*, the apprentice became a *Geselle*. The *Geselle* had to complete the *Walz*, a year of traveling from town to town, seeking temporary work from different *Meisters*.

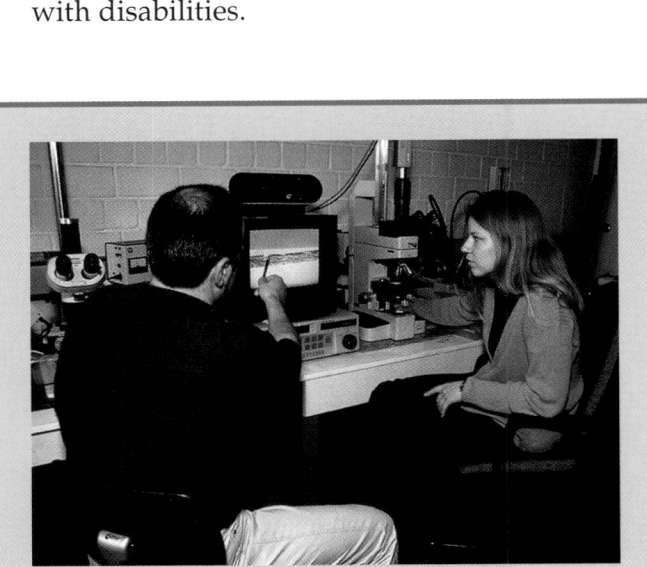

*Although the **Walz** is no longer common, Germans still get a lot of practical training as part of their education. This woman learns how to use optical equipment at the Darmstadt Technical University.*

Get active!

Many Germans love sports. About one-quarter of the population belongs to a sports club of some kind, and children belong to sports leagues which they attend after school. Germany has produced many famous athletes sports, such as Boris Becker in tennis and Katarina Witt in figure skating. Many of these athletes came from the former East Germany. Before reunification, East Germany spent a great deal of money to train athletes to become Olympic medal winners.

Around the countryside

Families hiking or cycling together are a common sight on weekends. Hiking trails are marked through forests, and many areas have scenic bicycle paths. Families also head north to the Baltic Sea or North Sea for a day of relaxing and swimming. During the summer, the beaches are packed!

(above) Hikers climb a ladder near the top of the rugged Zugspitze, Germany's tallest mountain.

(below) People rent wicker beach baskets on the North Sea Coast. The baskets provide a little shade and protection from the wind.

This snowboarder keeps his balance while going down a steep slope in the Bavarian Alps.

Fun in the snow

Winter sports are popular in Germany, especially in the south, where there is a lot of snow. The Bavarian Alps have perfect slopes for zipping down on a snowboard or on skis. Cross-country skiing is also very popular in the rolling hills of the lower mountains. Many towns in the mountains have their own ice rinks, ski jumps, and even bobsled runs, which are icy, twisting tracks that people slide down on sleds.

Fussball

Fussball, or soccer, is very popular in Germany. People play on any available patch of grass, and there are usually a number of neighborhood games being played in a single park.

When the national soccer team is playing, the excitement can be felt throughout the country. People in apartment buildings hang German flags from their balconies. The streets become deserted as fans watch the game at the stadium or on television. Some even travel to other countries to cheer for their team. When the German team wins, people pour into the streets waving flags and singing as passing cars honk their horns.

A relaxing soak

Mineral springs are found throughout Germany, especially in the mountains. Springs bubble up with fresh water that is sometimes very hot. The water contains minerals that are thought to heal aches and pains. People soak in the water, often staying at **spas** built around the springs.

Baden means "to bathe." Many German towns that have natural springs have names that begin with the word *Bad*. One of the most famous mineral springs, called Baden-Baden, is located in the southwest, near the Black Forest.

Leaving Germany

Germans are known for their love of travel. They often go away during their six weeks of vacation each year. Since Germany is located in the center of Europe, many countries are within a day's drive. Germans often load up their car and camp while on their holidays. They also travel to countries further away to enjoy and learn about different cultures.

People in front of the Cologne Cathedral watch in-line skaters perform daring tricks.

Clara's busy Saturday

"Clara, come on. Wake up!" says *Herr* Mueller, as he flicks the light switch on and off.

Clara pulls her cozy *Federbett*, a down-filled blanket, over her head. "But Papa, it's Saturday," she groans from her loft bed, high above the floor.

"Look, it's a quarter to six. I let you sleep for an extra fifteen minutes. Now, get up. You know that customers start coming early."

For days, the Muellers have been organizing their belongings in preparation for the monthly flea market. Many other families in the area around Chemnitz have been planning to sell their unwanted belongings, too. There is sure to be a lot of competition at the flea market this morning.

Clara hangs her feet over the edge of the bed, searching for the first rung of the ladder. She scrambles down and then rummages through her chest of drawers, built under her bed to save space. She gets ready quickly and hurries to the kitchen. After her rye bread pops out of the toaster, she covers it with hazelnut-chocolate spread. Clara finishes her glass of milk, brushes her teeth quickly, grabs her jacket, and races down the stairs.

Clara and her father pull out of the parking lot and head toward the center of Chemnitz. *Herr* Mueller struggles to get the car into third gear. The grinding gears make a terrible racket.

"Papa, when are we getting rid of this Trabbi?"

"I'm afraid this car might outlive both of us."

(left) Clara has a shower and brushes her teeth before rushing downstairs for breakfast.

(below) At the market, people bargain with each other to try to get the best price.

"But now that you've got your new job at the Volkswagen plant, can't we buy something better?"

The Muellers live in the area that was once East Germany. Clara's father used to work at a power station, where electricity was produced. Five years after reunification, the power station was shut down because it created too much pollution. Luckily, *Herr* Mueller was able to get a job with Volkswagen, which opened a new plant in the area.

Clara and her father set up their space at the market. The shoppers bargain with *Herr* Mueller. They try to get him to lower the price and they usually succeed. *Herr* Mueller and Clara have a successful morning. They manage to sell many paperback books, old sweaters, pots and pans — even Clara's old bicycle.

By 12:30 p.m., *Herr* Mueller and Clara are sitting at a picnic table, just off the market square, sharing a roast chicken that *Herr* Mueller bought at an *Imbiss*. When they are done, Clara and her father go shopping for groceries. They buy fresh bread at the *Bäckerei*, the bakery, and pork sausages at the *Metzgerei*, the butcher. They wander through an outdoor market where they choose some fruit and vegetables. Then, they head for the supermarket, where they buy the rest of the groceries, along with a bottle of *Riesling*, a German white wine from the Mosel Valley, as a surprise for Clara's mother.

When they return to the apartment, *Frau* Mueller is putting away her bicycle. She has been at their garden, a few blocks away, like many other apartment dwellers. She helps her husband unpack the groceries, while Clara flops in front of the television.

"Oh look," says *Frau* Mueller, "a lovely bottle of wine and a *Schwarzwäelderkirschtorte*!" "What!" cries Clara, as she comes racing in from the living room. "When did you buy that?" Her father had slipped into a *Konditorei*, while Clara was saving a picnic table and waiting for him to return with lunch. Black Forest cake is Clara's favorite. Clara and her parents all have some cake. Clara saves the cherries and chocolate shavings for last.

The phone rings for Clara. It is her friends, who are going to the local park to play soccer. Clara is tired and a little sick from eating so much rich food, but she changes into her shorts, grabs her soccer ball, and runs out to meet them anyway.

Clara and her father have trouble deciding what kind of sausages to buy for supper. There are so many different types to choose from.

 # Glossary

artisan A skilled craftsperson

au pair A person who moves to another country to work for a family in exchange for a place to live and a chance to learn a new language

braised Cooked by frying in oil and simmering in vinegar and spices

Christianity The Christian religion founded on the life and principles of Jesus Christ, who Christians believe to be the son of God

civilian A person who is not in military service

convert To change a person's religion, faith, or beliefs

descendant A person who can trace his or her family roots to a certain family or group

dictatorship A government in which there is one ruler who has complete power

discrimination The act of treating people unfairly because of race, religion, gender, or other factors

economy The organization and management of a country's businesses, industry, and money

ferment To change one substance into another through a chemical reaction

foothill A hill near the base of a mountain

massacre To kill a large number of people

occupy To invade and control a country, as by a foreign army

preservative Chemical substance that prevents food spoilage

pub A bar

Roman Catholic Church The Christian church, led by the Pope in Rome

spa A resort with special mineral baths

suburb A residential area outside a city

unified Joined together

worship To honor or respect a god

yeast A substance used in the production of beer, which changes sugar into alcohol and carbon dioxide

 # Index

1 2 3 4 5 6 7 8 9 0 Printed in the USA 0 9 8 7 6 5 4 3 2 1